The Mystery Of The Lost Customer

THE MYSTERY OF THE LOST CUSTOMER

Could high customer satisfaction be silently killing your business?

Susannah Simmons

Book Interior and E-book Design by
Amit Dey | amitdey2528@gmail.com

To find out more about our authors and books visit:
www.intellectualperspective.com

CONTENTS

PRAISE FOR THE MYSTERY OF THE LOST CUSTOMER

Having recently moved into the role of Assistant Director - Customer Success Management this book really resonated with me and I love the laidback style.

Shay Brannon, PassFort

A must-read for anyone striving to make their customers happier and more satisfied. Whether you're a business owner, manager, or professional seeking to elevate customer satisfaction, this book offers a wealth of knowledge, humor, clarity, real-life examples, and actionable insights. Unlock the secrets to customer happiness and watch your business thrive.

Peter Nuhn, Founder of x-focus, Powered by Responsibility

If you have bolts that need nuts threaded on, then it does not matter how fancy the hammer is, it still won't work. Susannah's P.E.R.M.E.A.T.E. model will help you understand what your customers and employees really need to create success. Full disclosure: I have been an accountability buddy for Susannah as she created this book.

Dan Kowalski,
Solution Instigator and author of
W.I.S.E. CHOICES AT WORK Go from doubting to DECISIVE when the clock is ticking

The most captivating and unusual business book I've read this year. Unlike typical business literature, this one captures your attention like a mystery novel, compelling you to flip pages quickly, seeking solutions and revelations at every turn. A refreshing and thought-provoking read that has a way of upending long-standing beliefs about customer satisfaction. Susannah Simmons has crafted an engaging story that is as enlightening as it is entertaining.

Debbie Jenkins, Asset Creation Coach and
author of *Stop Writing Books Nobody Reads* and
Stop Selling Books Nobody Buys

This is a book for all business owners as it really made me think beyond the immediate client to the people using the product. As a training business owner, I have wrestled with balancing the needs/expectations of the client, who commissions, with the participants that I work with but I've never had it explained so clearly why this can be hard before! And thinking about the wider impact of 'selling a product'. Susannah takes us on such a lively journey using a story which is entertaining and thought provoking. Her images are fabulous and bring home that any product has to survive contact with real workplaces.

Dr. Emma Williams, Director and
Chief Coffee Drinker at EJW Solutions Ltd.

Susannah Simmons breaks through the common and limited 'give them a great customer experience' perspective and broadens it to a more holistic approach in this fascinating and intriguing story of the lost customer. If your customers are disappearing, you'll want to implement the more encompassing and thoughtful approach presented in this book. This is not just another business book. It is a story that happens to be incredibly applicable to today's business world, where one needs to go beyond just providing a great customer (or user) experience. Learn how in this relevant book.

Carma Baughman, Instructional Designer
and UX/UI Career Coach

There were so many gems in this book that lead to action. I found myself applying the insights to my own onboarding processes for my different programs. More than that it made me truly consider different onboarding models for different types of course participants. That has been powerful and will ultimately contribute to the greater success of my programs. Thank you Susannah. Powerful and usable insights delivered in an accessible way!

Finola Howard, Creator & Founder at
How Great Marketing Works

I loved this book and the way in which Susannah cleverly used true stories to get her message across. She clearly lays out a common scenario that faces so many people today. The world is getting more complicated and noisy, not less and our businesses and teams are faced with extraordinary challenges. We all need this book to help us navigate our way through the stormy seas and find the safe harbour of wellbeing that we are searching for!

Sally Murphy, Founder at Welltold

Susannah crafts an accessible stealth textbook, in the form of an easy-to-read conversational, small but mighty business book. As a business owner, The Mystery Of The Lost Customer, gave me a new way to view my business through the lens of its functioning wellbeing. The genius model of 'PERMEATE' will encourage you to approach your business from a wellbeing point of view – what a great takeaway plus all those resources! A trainer's dream.

Anna Marsden, Trainer & Coach at
Luminescence Communications

PROLOGUE

1. "I had no #$@&%*! idea!"

"You look like you've had a bad day!" I said to Fin as they arrived at my house.

"I've had better days that's for sure. I lost a customer today totally out of the blue."

"Oh, that's rough. No warning signs at all?"

"Nope. Nothing. I had no #$@&%*! idea!"

"You better come in, have a drink and tell me all about it."

"Thanks."

Fin and I are old friends from the University of Plymouth where we both took business studies. Normally when we get together we talk about our families, holidays, what we've been watching on Netflix. This time, as you will read, it was slightly different.

"What's the story?" I asked once we were settled on the sofa, drinks in hand.

"As you know, I started a new job as a customer success manager at Headsets R Us last year. It has been going really well. My customers like me, my NPS[1] scores are good, I'm on track with my sales target, so my boss is happy."

"Go on."

"Well today I followed up with one of my customers. I sold them some of our leading brand headsets about a month ago and there was an opportunity for more sales. They have about 250 employees but only placed an initial order for fifteen headsets. So, I called my customer who gave me an NPS score of 10 on the previous sale. When I last checked in they told me everyone was loving the award-winning product, so I definitely thought there was a sales opportunity. I'd told the boss as much and added it the sales forecast. More fool me!"

"I'm guessing your customer didn't place another order?"

"Worse than that. They said 'Sorry Fin. We won't be buying any more headsets from Headsets R Us. We've changed supplier.'"

"Ah!"

"Just like that. Customer lost. Like I said, I had no #$@&%*! idea and I've got no explanation for my boss."

"I'm sorry you've had a tough day and lost a customer. I wonder whether Headsets R Us are suffering from a Silent Killer."

2. "Silent Killers in business?"

Fin looks at me with a puzzled expression.

"Silent Killer – what on earth are you talking about?"

"You're familiar with the concept of a Silent Killer when it comes to our health, right?"

"Of course. Things like high blood pressure, high blood sugar and, of course, your personal nemesis, cholesterol. See I do listen to you harping on about this stuff!"[2]

Silent Killer: a disease that has no obvious symptoms or indications

"I'm not sure I harp on but thanks." I smile. "So anyway, this idea of things that we can't see but could be putting our health at risk. I applied it to business and asked myself: what are the potential Silent Killers destroying the health of organisations and putting them at risk?"

"And what did you come up with?"

"Wellbeing of course!

"Of course," Fin replied rolling their eyes with a smirk. "You mean employee wellbeing? Like rest areas, mental health first aiders, that kind of thing? I don't see what that has to do with my customer dropping me like a stone."

"No, I don't mean that, and don't get me started on some companies' efforts to improve employee wellbeing!"

"What do you mean then?"

"I mean customer, user and employee wellbeing and how they aren't mutually exclusive. I mean thinking beyond experience."

3. Experience vs wellbeing

"When I did a search on Amazon.com, within Books, there were over 4,000 results for employee experience, over 7,000 for customer experience and over 10,000 results for user experience. Experience is clearly a big topic."

"Agreed. My boss is always going to events and reading stuff on customer experience."

"Well consider a typical dictionary definition of an experience: '**An event or occurrence which leaves an impression on someone**.' To me, an event or occurrence suggests a single point in time, not something lasting. Compare this with the definition of wellbeing: '**the state of being comfortable, healthy or happy**'. The use of the word 'state' suggests longevity, something lasting. Isn't that what we want in business? A lasting positive state as a result of using our products and services and interacting with our employees."

"Yeah, I guess so," replied Fin unconvincingly.

"Unfortunately, the focus on experience could drive us to think about user, customer and employee journeys just in terms of touchpoints and creating 'wow moments' or 'happiness hits'. I am not saying this is a bad thing. However, suspend judgement for a moment and consider the idea that focusing on user experience, customer experience and employee experience isn't enough."

"You mean 3X doesn't guarantee success."

"Exactly, I'm going to pinch that." I smiled. "Ask yourself what business success could look like if you thought about those three journeys in terms of creating a positive state, consistently and sustainably, over someone's lifetime with your business whether as a user, a customer or an employee (or perhaps all three!). What if we made wellbeing the goal?"

"A nice idea, but how does that work in practice?"

"It is probably easiest using the example of one of my recent customers. But first let me explain a bit more about wellbeing."

"Sure. Go ahead."

4. PERMA™: A model for human flourishing

"Your company's employees, customers and users are all human."

"Debatable sometimes!" laughed Fin.

"Now, now! With this in mind, a model for human wellbeing seems like a good place to start. Martin Seligman, a pioneer in positive psychology and author of *Flourish*[3], states that human wellbeing can be defined and measured using five elements. People will derive wellbeing from each of these blocks to varying degrees.

"The five elements are:

Positive Emotion – experiencing Positive Emotions such as joy, gratitude and contentment.

Engagement – being fully engaged and absorbed in activities that we find enjoyable and Meaningful.

Relationships – having positive Relationships with others, including close and supportive connections with friends, family and community.

Meaning – having a sense of purpose and Meaning in life, and feeling that our actions are contributing to something larger than ourselves.

Accomplishment – setting and achieving goals, and feeling a sense of Accomplishment and mastery over our lives.

"The goal of wellbeing theory is to promote something called human flourishing. Human flourishing represents a vision of human life in which individuals are able to realise their full potential and achieve a sense of Meaningful and satisfying existence, whilst also contributing to the well-being of others and the world around them. What if we applied this idea to business and the goal of business well-being theory was to promote business flourishing? Where business flourishing represents a vision for business life in which organisations are able to realise their full potential and achieve a sense of Meaningful existence, whilst also contributing to the wellbeing of others and the world around them."

"Sounds awesome. Go on," said Fin, leaning in to learn more.

5. PERMEATE™: A model for business flourishing

"Whilst Seligman's model is a useful starting point, I believe it has some core elements missing that are important for business flourishing. Allow me to introduce you to PERMEATE™: a model for a flourishing business.

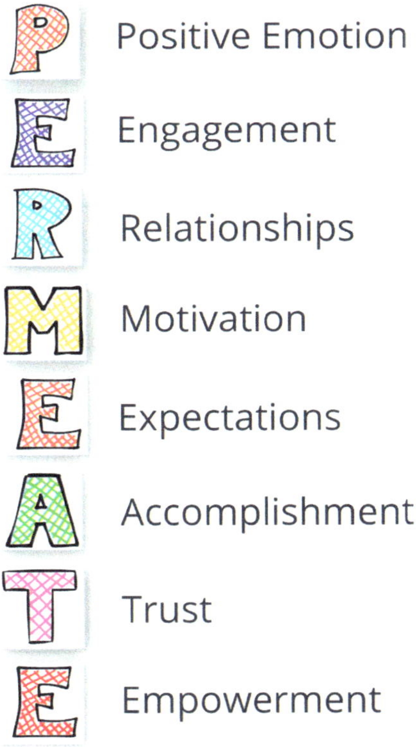

"My model keeps Seligman's first element of **Positive Emotion.** It focuses on the pleasant life; how happy someone would say they are. Positive Emotion is often triggered by events or occurrences so it links nicely to the idea of an experience that a customer, user or employee might have. However, this route to wellbeing has limitations. Firstly, we are limited by our disposition. Many people are low in experiencing Positive Emotion, and for all of us our emotions tend to fluctuate within a range. Secondly, Positive Emotion is short-lived. It is unrealistic to believe that we can live life on a permanent 'high'. These highs are caused by spikes in our 'happiness hormones', primarily dopamine, and our bodies cannot sustain those levels for long periods."

"It's like when people get a pay rise. They are happy for a while and then it wears off," interrupted Fin.

"That's a great example. And actually this is compounded by the research that has investigated the diminishing returns of earning more money. Whilst an employee might feel happy going from 30k to 60k a year, earning another 30k won't have the same impact. To get the same dopamine hit, they need to double their income again to 120k. What's more, as income rises to a certain threshold where certain needs are met, satisfaction diminishes.[3] This is just one example that supports why we need to consider other routes to wellbeing beyond Positive Emotion or experience."

"So what's the second element of your model?"

"Engagement is also included in my model. Can you think of a time when you have been so absorbed in an activity that it has felt like time has stopped?"

"Playing on my games console," Fin grinned.

"I could have guessed," I smiled. "This is what Mihaly Csikszentmihalyi, another leading name in positive psychology, calls 'flow' and this is what Engagement is. People who experience flow or 'being in the zone' report a deep sense of enjoyment, satisfaction and fulfilment from their activities. The characteristics of flow include a clear sense of goals and feedback, a balance between the challenge level of the task and our skills, a sense of control over the situation, and a loss of self-consciousness and time awareness."

"It would be great if this is how people felt every time they used our products and services!"

"Exactly! The third element is still **Relationships**."

"Understandable. I don't think anyone would disagree that they are fundamental to business success, particularly customer loyalty and lifetime value."

"Agreed. Products and services have the power to build, or destroy human Relationships. Sounds a bit dramatic but consider this. Our experiences are often amplified through our Relationships. So when people use our products and services, we want it to add value to Relationships, to improve how they feel about themselves, about each other and their interactions. Feeling connected to other people, feeling part of an 'in-group', feeling safe with others, feeling someone has their interests at heart and is interested in them; these are all things we can influence on the user, customer and employee journey."

"So thinking back to my games console, whilst it has a positive impact on my Positive Emotion and Engagement it could be negatively impacting Relationships because of how my partner feels about it?"

"Yep."

"Hmm, interesting. Carry on."

"M is where I start to deviate from Seligman's model. My M is for **Motivation** rather than Meaning. Whilst some products and services can contribute to someone's Meaning and help them achieve their purpose in life the links can be tenuous and difficult to find. My intention is for this model to be useful, practical and easy to apply. Motivation plays a crucial role in driving human behaviour and goal achievement. Understanding the factors that influence it can be essential to personal growth, wellbeing and success. This understanding can also be used to inform business decisions and processes."

"Are we back to pay rises again?"

"No. People have a tendency to focus on extrinsic motivators like money, gifts and recognition and forget about intrinsic motivators. We could have a separate conversation about Motivation but we both need to get up for work tomorrow. I will send you the link to an interview I did with someone who specialises in Motivation if you're interested."

"Definitely!"

You can watch this video too.
TheMysteryOfTheLostCustomer.com/Resources

"Next we have E for **Expectations**. Our brains are constantly in search of information. Research conducted by Broomberg-Martin and Hikosaka (2009)[4] suggests that not only do our brains want information, but the sooner we get it, the better. Furthermore, research from Wiggins et al.[5] found that people prefer negative information to no information."

"It's like when you are stuck on a train that isn't moving and they don't tell you what's happening. So frustrating. That's not good for my wellbeing!"

"I know, right?! Having bad news means people are able to get on and plan. When it comes to products and services, setting (and resetting) expectations about what is going to happen, when it's going to happen and who is responsible, can have a huge impact on user, customer and employee wellbeing and therefore the success of products and businesses.

"**Accomplishment** is in Seligman's model and still has its place here. In the context of this idea of business flourishing it refers to our users, customers and employees working towards, and achieving, goals. It also includes mastery and competence. People pursue achievement, competence, success, and mastery for their own sakes, in a variety of domains, including the workplace, sports, games, and hobbies. They pursue it even when it does not necessarily lead to Positive Emotion, Meaning or Relationships. In my opinion it is not enough to just consider how our products and services help our customers and users accomplish something or improve their mastery and competence at a task. We also need to think about how our employees influence that Accomplishment.

"**Trust** is the next element in my model. For me Trust is a keystone in both human and business wellbeing. There is a very good reason why "lack of Trust" is the foundation of Lencioni's *The Five Dysfunctions of a Team*.[6] Trust is a fundamental aspect of human Relationships and interaction and is essential for building strong, positive and fulfilling connections with others. However, it is not just the human interactions that can build or damage Trust.

Interactions with products and services themselves can also impact a user and customer's Trust. In their 2022 Trust Report,[7] Adobe reported that 57% of consumers say that once a company has violated their Trust they will never give that company their business again. That is a huge risk to businesses who fail to live up to their promises and customer expectations."

"I agree Trust is really important although I don't think I damaged the Trust with my customer which is why I am so stumped."

"Perhaps it is a breakdown in Trust elsewhere that you can't see. Like the breakdown in Trust my customer had. My model has just one more element before we get to their story.

"The final element is **Empowerment**. This refers to the process of enabling individuals or groups to take control of their lives, make their own decisions and act on their own behalf. It requires providing people with the skills, resources and opportunities they need to achieve their goals, overcome obstacles and, therefore, improve their wellbeing and quality of life. It is about genuinely allowing users, customers and employees to make autonomous decisions about what to do, when and how.

"That's the full model so now for my customer's story. But first a comfort break."

"Good idea. I'll top up the drinks and snacks too."

Endnotes

1. Net Promoter Score, or NPS, is used by companies to measure customer experience and predict business growth. The score is calculated by asking customers to score on a scale of zero to ten how likely they are to recommend the brand, product or service to a friend or colleague. The scores are used to group respondents into one of three categories: promoters, passives and detractors. The NPS score is calculated by subtracting the percentage of detractors from the percentage of promoters.

2. I have another business as the Feel Good Fitness Coach, and I am passionate about inspiring, motivating and supporting people to take care of their health and fitness.

3. Seligman, M. *Flourish: A New Understanding of Happiness and Well-being - and How to Achieve them,* 2011, Nicholas Brealey Publishing

4. According to the research article *High income improves evaluation of life but not emotional well-being* published by Daniel Kahneman and Angus Deaton in 2010 (Proceedings of the National Academy of Sciences), the "certain threshold" where satisfaction starts to diminish is $75,000. Today, in 2023, the satiation point is considered to be higher and researchers continue to investigate and debate the question "does money make us happy?"

5. Broomberg-Martin, E S and Hikosaka, O (2009) Midbrain dopamine neurons signal preference for advance information about upcoming rewards, *Neuron*, 63 (1), pp 119–26

6. Wiggins, S et al. (1991) The psychological consequence of predictive testing for Huntingdon's disease, *New England Journal of Medicine*, 327 (20), pp 1401–05

7. Lencioni, P. *The Five Dysfunctions of a Team*, First Edition, John Wiley & Sons

8. Adobe, *Trust Report The digital economy is personal*, https://business.adobe.com/uk/resources/reports/adobe-trust-report.html

ACT I: THE CUSTOMER OR CUSTOMERS?

6. Uma the user

Feeling refreshed Fin and I settle on the sofa and begin the story of Uma.

"Picture the scene. There has been a global pandemic that meant everyone had to stay in their houses and limit their in-person contact with other people. Virtual meeting platforms saw a boom in business and, whilst people have now returned to their offices, hybrid working and virtual meetings are here to stay."

"Well, that's obviously not hard to imagine," said Fin.

"This is the situation Uma found themself in and they were having a nightmare. Uma worked in a customer-facing role and had regular calls with colleagues and customers. There weren't enough meeting rooms for the number of virtual meetings everyone was having so Uma had to sit at their desk or a breakout area. There was too much background noise, customers were complaining that they couldn't hear and the whole environment was distracting. What do you think Uma's wellbeing was like?"

"It probably wasn't very good."

"And thinking about it from the perspective of PERMEATE?

"I imagine all elements of PERMEATE were scoring low. There was little Positive Emotion, whilst feeling frustrated and distracted. As Uma was not able to get into flow, there was a lack of Engagement. Relationships with colleagues and customers were negatively impacted. They were probably not feeling Motivated because they were not Accomplishing the job to the standard they would like and not meeting their own or others' Expectations. The Trust in Uma's ability to do the job effectively will have been diminishing. Not only Uma's Trust but also their colleagues' and customers'. Uma possibly felt out of control in this situation and unempowered. I've probably just described exactly why lots of my customers come to me for our headsets because their employees are in the same situation."

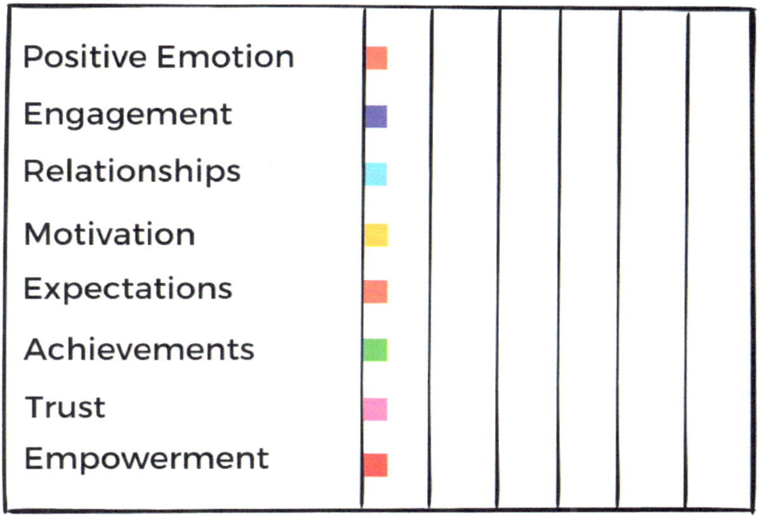

"Great. I knew you would be able to relate to this example. So, Uma, having had enough, and not feeling completely unempowered, decided to take action by going to see Clem in the IT department. Upon hearing Uma's tale of woe Clem said, 'No worries. I'll get you a noise cancelling headset. You'll be able to do your meetings at your desk, no problem. You'll be able to hear the customers. They'll be able to hear you and they won't be able to hear the background noise of the office. We'll get it sorted in no time.' Uma left feeling relieved and couldn't wait for the headset to arrive."

"Nice deposit into the emotional bank account!"

"Exactly! I didn't know you knew about the emotional bank account."

"You told me. It has been really useful and I use it a lot. Although I probably need to think about how playing on my games console impacts my partner's emotional bank account."

Discover more about The Power of the Emotional Bank Account at TheMysteryOfTheLostCustomer.com/Resources

---

"Indeed! Back to the story. Clem immediately phoned Sam, their usual supplier, and described Uma's predicament. It was a familiar story and Sam had just the thing for Clem. 'Oh, we've got an award-winning noise-cancelling headset. It's brilliant. You're going to love it. It's got all this fantastic functionality, all the whistles and bells.' 'Brilliant!' said Clem, 'That sounds like an amazing product. Just what we need.' So Clem ordered some of these best in class noise cancelling headsets. Clem hadn't got the budget, or authority, to order a headset for all staff in the organisation so placed an order for fifteen. 'I'll get one for Uma, one for everyone in the IT team and a few spare.' Sam processed the order and arranged delivery. When the delivery arrived the headsets got put away in the IT cupboard."

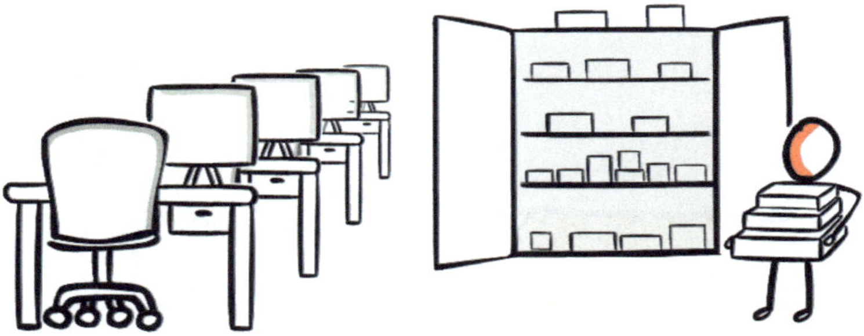

"Wait what about Uma?! The headset isn't going to improve Uma's wellbeing if it is sat in an IT cupboard."

"You're not wrong. I like to think of a product like medicine. People will only get the benefits if they actually use it."

"Thinking about it, Uma's wellbeing may even have declined because they thought Clem was going to fix the problem but hasn't. That won't have helped build Trust."

"Yep. You are starting to see the Silent Killers."

"I am, but that's not Sam's fault. What can Sam do?"

"Don't worry, we will get to that."

7. Clem the customer

"Let's turn our attention to Clem, Sam's customer. After receiving the delivery of the headsets Clem received an email from Sam asking for feedback. Clem scored Sam 10 out of 10 and left a comment 'The customer experience was fabulous, service was fast, really friendly, love it! Great supplier, we love working with you. 10 out of 10 every time.'"

"Well done, Sam; although Uma still wouldn't have been happy!"

"Indeed, so you won't be surprised to hear that a week or so later Clem got a disgruntled message from Uma asking for an update on the headset. Clem apologised and told Uma that the headsets had arrived and one would be dropped round later that day. Clem got the headsets out of the cupboard, handed them out to the IT team and dropped one on Uma's desk on their way out for lunch."

"Did Clem speak to Uma?"

"No, Uma was already out on lunch. When Clem came back they walked past Uma and saw that they were using the new headset. The IT team had been using theirs all morning too. When Sam called later that afternoon to check in, Clem said, 'We are doing great. Uma has their headset. We love ours in the IT team. We can understand why it is an award-winning product. So many great whistles and bells.' Sam is very pleased to hear this and asked Clem whether there might be interest in buying more headsets for other employees. Clem was sure there would be and told Sam to call back in a month."

"Sam was in exactly the same position as me. Thinks everything is great and there is an opportunity for more sales. But you're going to tell me that wasn't the case, aren't you?"

"I'm afraid so. Unfortunately, what Clem (and Sam) were unaware of was Uma's continuing frustration. Uma was out in the corridor, head in hands, close to tears. When a colleague asked if they were okay they exclaimed,

'Award-winning headset my foot! It doesn't connect properly in the meeting platform. Half the time the sound comes out of the laptop speakers and people can't hear me. Then, to top it all off, when it was working I pressed a button thinking it would mute me and it disconnected the call.[8] I am so embarrassed! I just wanted to plug the headset in and it to work.' I think you will agree that at this point Uma's wellbeing hadn't improved despite using the product."

"I can imagine that some elements of PERMEATE have dropped even further like Relationships, Motivation, Trust and Empowerment."

"Uma would definitely agree with that. Despite having, and using, the headset Uma's wellbeing hadn't improved. Therefore I revise my statement from earlier and say that your product is like medicine. People will only get the benefits if they use it 'according to directions.'"

8. Harry the head of department

Fin sat back looking thoughtful.

"I presume Sam, like me, didn't get the additional sale and lost the customer?"

"Yep."

"But surely the experience of one user, Uma, didn't have the power or influence to lose Sam the business? IT were responsible for ordering headsets, the IT team loved theirs and Sam was the existing supplier who sounded like they had a great product."

"If I tell you the rest of the story perhaps you will see how Uma's wellbeing did have the power and influence to lose Sam the business."

"Yep, please do, I'm intrigued."

"Allow me to introduce Harry, a head of department. At their regular department meeting, the team raised that they too were struggling to adapt to the new, hybrid world and were having similar issues to Uma with their online meetings. One member of the team said 'Uma got a new headset recently. I think IT ordered it.' Another colleague said, 'Oh no, don't get the one Uma's got. All I hear is moans about it. In fact, I think they've given up using it. We don't want those, definitely don't want those!' Harry wanted to get on with the meeting so wrapped up the discussion. 'I appreciate we need to have better calling experiences with our customers. Leave it with me. I'll look into it and get back to you.'

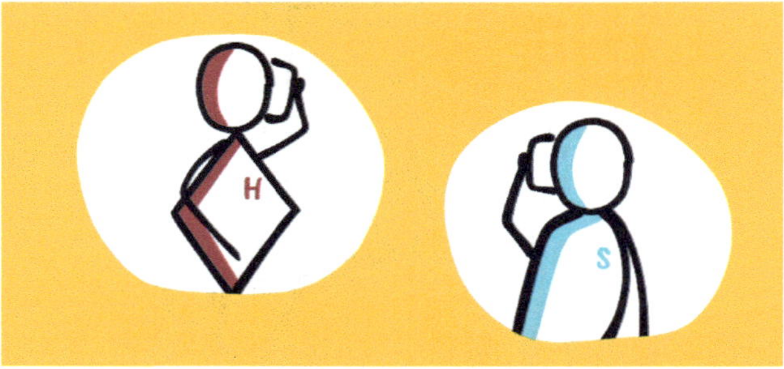

"Harry is a great manager who follows through on commitments and wants the best for their team. However, instead of going to Clem in IT, Harry called a supplier they used at a previous company. After asking some questions, the supplier recommended a middle of the range product that didn't have as many whistles and bells as their top-end product, but explained to Harry that it would be perfect for their needs. Easy to use and compatible with their meeting platform. Harry was delighted and had the budget, and authority, to order one for each member of the team. Delivery was arranged in time for the next department meeting.

"At that meeting, Harry handed out the new headsets and used time in the meeting to share details of additional resources the supplier had provided to help them get started. Harry's team were thrilled with their headsets and most of them were up and running straight after the meeting. A couple of people had issues, but the supplier had given them details of how they could get help, and these were quickly resolved."

"No user wellbeing issues for these folks then?!"

"Nope and what do you think Uma's reaction was when they walked past Harry's team and saw them all having a great experience with their headsets?"

"Not impressed I imagine."

"That's right. At the next senior leadership team meeting Harry was asked about the headsets. Based on the experience of Harry's team it was agreed that they would switch supplier for all future headsets. Harry passed on the supplier's details to the head of IT who asked Clem to work with each of the heads of departments to get headsets ordered."

"And that is how Uma the user's wellbeing silently killed Sam's business!"

"That's right! It wasn't the first time either and that's why they asked me for help."

Endnotes

1. This actually happened to me and it was quite embarrassing. I had been given a laptop and wired headset by a client for use during a project. Nobody had given me any information to get me up and running quickly and effectively with my new equipment. I learned by doing and sometimes that isn't always the best way. That said I didn't make the same mistake again.

ACT II:
THE SUPPLIER

9. "But I got a 10 on the NPS score"

Fin leaned back on the sofa. "Let me get this straight. Sam's company is your customer?"

"Yep."

"How do you know all about Uma, Clem and Henry?"

"You mean Harry," I said, smiling. "I've met Sam's boss, the head of customer success, a few times, and after the situation with Clem, they decided enough was enough and gave me a call. Like I said this wasn't the first time a customer had taken their business elsewhere. And it was having an impact on the customer success team's wellbeing, particularly as their measures of success include customer retention and repeat business."

"I can totally relate to that. A customer leaving doesn't do much for Positive Emotion, Engagement and Motivation, and not hitting targets is the opposite of Accomplishment! How did you help them?"

"First of all I asked if they could get me access to the customer that had left. Fortunately, the relationship was good enough that they could, and I was able to interview Clem first. That prompted me to spend time talking with Uma and Harry. I then facilitated several workshops with Sam's team to help them use what I had uncovered to make improvements to their processes."

"How did that go down?"

"It was tough to start with, particularly for Sam who was still quite emotional about losing the customer. All they kept saying at the start was 'But I got a 10 on the NPS score'."

"How did you handle it?"

"I asked Sam who had given them the 10..."

"Clem."

"And then I asked, based on the information I had gathered, what score they thought Uma would have given them?"

"Well initially Uma would have said, 'What headset?!'"

"Exactly. I asked Sam how they knew that Uma had got their headset, and Sam said, 'Well I assumed Clem had given it to them.'"

"We all know what assume did![9] So that was the first lesson. Like you said before, just because the customer has received the product don't assume they are using it."

"Yes, and following on from that, **not all customers are users and not all users are customers**."

"And there might even be multiple customers, or prospective customers, because actually Harry was the customer who bought from the competitor initially. I can see that thinking of a customer as just the company could Silently Kill your business. It is the people within those companies that decide to buy so when we think of customers that is who we need to be considering."

"Spot on. This is why identifying key stakeholders and managing them based on their power or influence and their interest in your product is so important. Want to have a go at the activity I did with Sam and the team?"

"Sure."

I grabbed a pen and paper and drew the grid of the Power Interest Matrix[10] and asked Fin, "At the start of the story, where would you place Uma on the grid?"

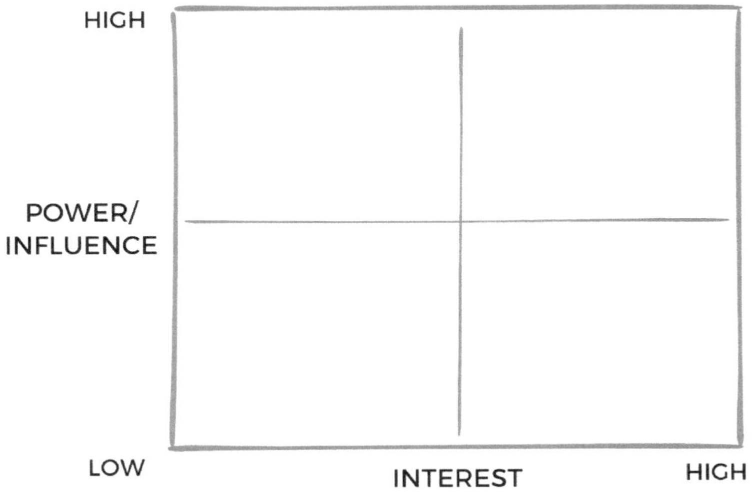

"I would have said low power but definitely high interest so bottom right-hand box"

"Where would you have put Clem?"

"Probably top-right, high power and high interest."

"And Harry the head of department whose team might be having the same issues as Uma?"

"Hmm probably high power and at the start of the story low interest but later, when the team raised their issues in the team meeting, high interest."

"Great observation which highlights that stakeholder needs are dynamic therefore stakeholder analysis isn't a 'one and done' exercise because stakeholders can change and their levels of power and interest can change."

"You could even argue that Uma's power increased the more unhappy they became. So presumably each box has a different label for how you should manage the stakeholder."

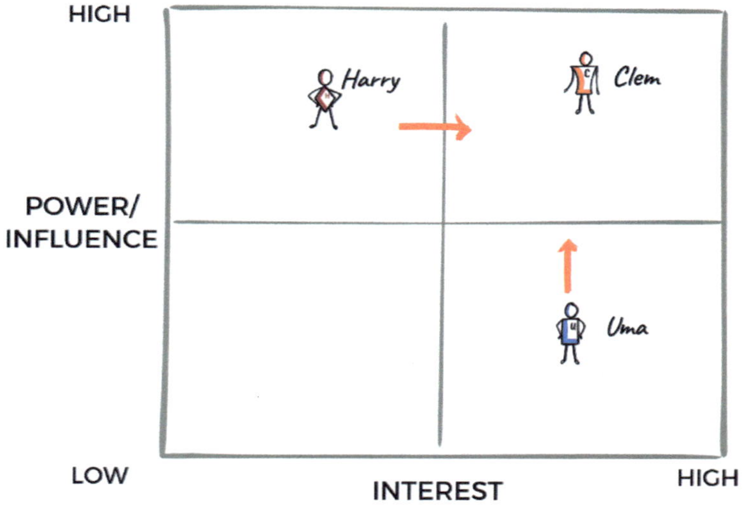

"It does." And I wrote the labels from the classic model on the grid. "You'll notice that Harry would have been in the 'Keep Satisfied' group and Uma would have been 'Keep Informed' and that doesn't seem right to me."

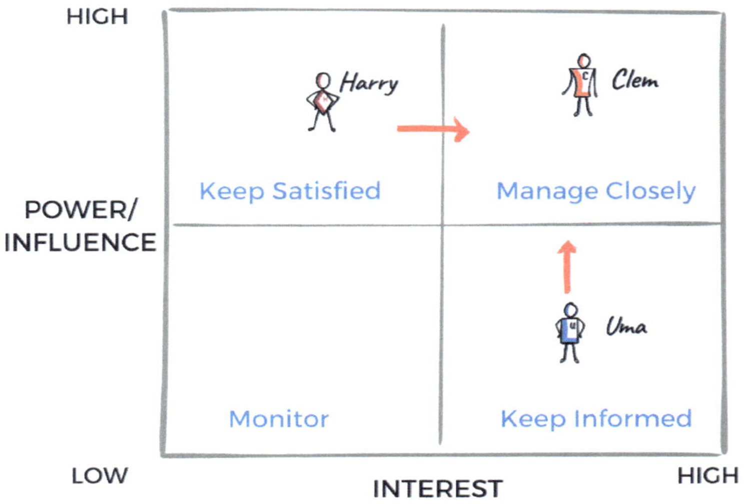

"Yeah, based on Uma's story you want the product users to be satisfied not just informed if you want to maximise all the elements of PERMEATE."

"That's exactly why I have adapted the model from four quadrants to three zones:

- Monitor for low power/influence and interest
- Anticipate and Meet Needs for high power/influence or interest
- Manage Closely for high power/influence and interest."

"How about adding arrows as well to show the dynamic nature of the model?" Fin asked thoughtfully.

"Love it and I will call it The Power-Interest Dynamics Map!"

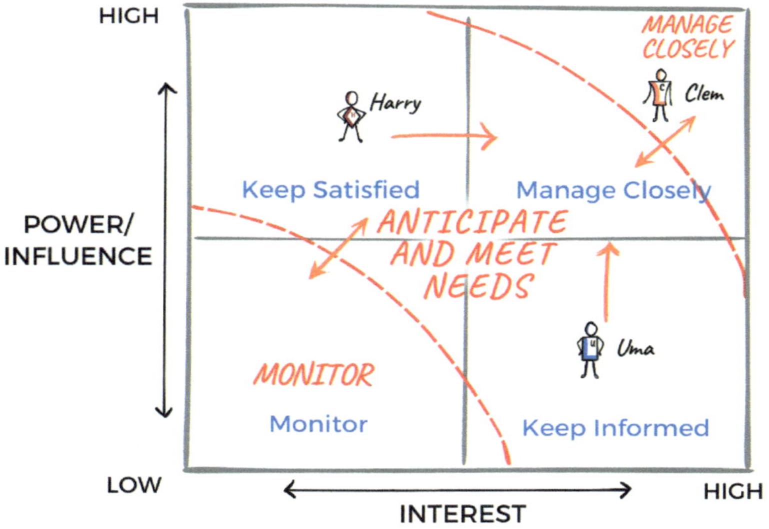

Fin sat staring at the piece of paper. "That reminds me of another situation I had with a customer."

"Go on."

"Purchasing. I had a customer who almost didn't place an additional order because the cost would mean getting the purchasing team involved and potentially putting it out to tender despite us supplying them for years. Fortunately, we had a good enough relationship with our main contact that they told us, and we could work together to avoid that. Up until that point purchasing hadn't been on my radar but now I will monitor that team more closely because if things like their policies and procedures change their power and interest may increase."

"Another Silent Killer?"

"Yes. You know I can really see how other stakeholders could Silently Kill our business."

"And that could be true of any customer so I would always have certain departments like purchasing and finance included on the map even if they always sit in the monitor zone. The worst example I had of another stakeholder damaging user wellbeing was as the customer. It was for a new learning management system, and I was one of the user representatives on the project team. We had done a really thorough requirements gathering exercise and vendor selection process. When it came to negotiating the price and signing the contract we had to pass it to Purchasing. They asked our chosen supplier if they had something cheaper. To which they said yes and offered the off-the-shelf product that wasn't fit for our needs at all. The project team and all the users had to find a way to make it work. Let's just say user wellbeing hit rock bottom for a while; to the point that people left the company."

"Wow! Sounds like fun times."

"It was definitely a learning experience and played a part in why I do what I do today."

"This is probably a silly question, but do you have a copy of the Power-Interest Dynamics Map that I can use as a template?"

"You should know by now that I don't believe there is such a thing as a silly question," I teased, "and yes, I do have a template. I will send you the link."

Download your own copy of the Power-Interest Dynamics Map at TheMysteryOfTheLostCustomer.com/Resources

---

10. "The IT team didn't have any problems."

"Did Sam have a hard time accepting anything else?" Fin enquired.

"There were a couple of other things that came up," I replied. "After hearing Uma's story, Sam accepted how Harry's decision to use another supplier had come about and that the only stakeholder that was being managed was Clem. We moved on to discuss the customer and user journey and I started to draw this pictogram. We ultimately got talking about Uma's onboarding experience."

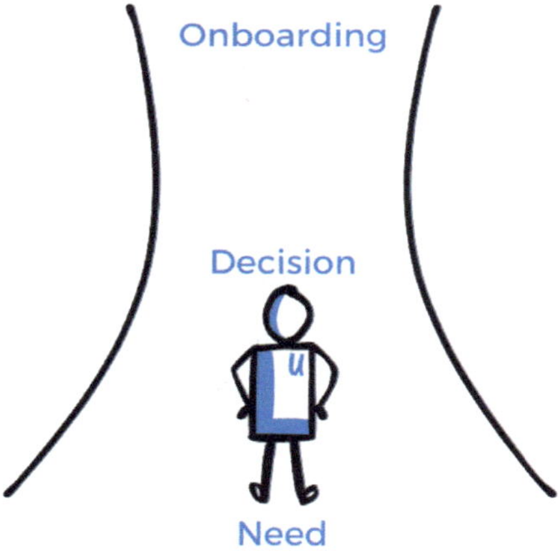

"You mean Clem leaving the headset on Uma's desk whilst they were out at lunch?!"

"That's the one. I posed the question, 'What could you, as the supplier, have done differently to help Clem provide Uma with a better onboarding experience?' Sam protested, 'Why should we need to? The IT team didn't have any problems and they loved the headsets.'"

"Hang on though," interrupted Fin. "I don't want to stereotype but isn't there a high probability that the members of the IT team are tech geeks and more familiar, and comfortable, with the features of the headset. Perhaps Uma wasn't?"

"This was exactly the case here, and it was the next lesson for Sam and the team. **Not all users are the same**. It highlights the importance of understanding the typical categories of product users and creating user personas. Creating user personas helps an organisation put end users at the centre of the conversation and provide context for why the product will be used and what value it can create."

"I have heard people talking about user stories. Are those the same thing?" Fin asked.

"User stories are written about each persona. With Sam's team we identified the personas then used that information to create the story. Stories are often expressed as persona plus need plus purpose so in sentence form 'As (persona), I (want to), (so that). Have a try for Uma?'

"Okay," Fin said reluctantly. "Hmmm... As Uma, I want to be able to easily connect my headset to my laptop and it work seamlessly in virtual meetings so that I can quickly and easily communicate with my customer."

"Great!"

"But wait a minute. Isn't this the responsibility of product development? Aren't they supposed to test and make sure products do what they're supposed to?"

"That's exactly what Sam's colleague asked, and yes you are right. However, there are variables that a product design team can't control like how the user uses the product, the context it is used in and the user's previous experience and attitude towards that type of product or even the brand. If we return to the analogy from earlier that your product is like medicine. People will only get the benefits if they use it 'according to directions'. We are relying on people being given those directions and following them. Some of these elements can be picked up along the user journey and addressed during onboarding."

"What you're really trying to say is that they can't design out user error?! What's that saying they use in IT?"

"Oh, you mean a problem between the chair and the keyboard?" I chuckled. "Or PICNIC, Problem in Chair, Not in Computer."

"That's the one," laughed Fin.

"All joking aside, by thinking about user personas in the context of onboarding we can anticipate some of those 'problems in the chair' and put things in place to minimise the impact and maximise the user's wellbeing."

"What did you get Sam's team to think about when you were working with them on user personas?"

"First of all we had to consider that everyone is different in terms of their skills, experience, interests, time pressures and job role for example. These will all have an influence on how a product is received. Whilst we can't create a user persona for every single prospective user we can create them for typical categories like I said before."

"Like Uma and the IT Team."

"Yes, and that is where we started. I got Sam's team to put themselves in Uma's shoes and then in the shoes of someone from the IT team. It was important to take time to consider both the personality traits of the user and the context in which they will be using the product, and then what help they might need whilst using the product."

"Presumably you are having to make a lot of assumptions?" asked Fin, "and we've already said assumptions are bad."

"Making assumptions isn't bad necessarily if you are conscious of them and you make time to challenge them. This process can help inform your decision-making about the choices you offer customers. For example, Uma spends a lot of time on the phone speaking to customers. That is why she needs a decent headset. You might assume that to get help with the product she would want access to a telephone helpline because that is her preferred method of communication. In fact, when I spoke to her, her preference was to use live chat and she doesn't particularly like using the phone."

"That's probably another reason why the headset experience had such a negative impact on her wellbeing."

"Yes, it was and that is why I got Sam's team to think about the user personas in relation to PERMEATE. They had to think about how each element of the model could be addressed for that user in the context that the product would be used. I can send you the output from the exercise if it would be helpful."

"That would be great. You're not going to charge me a consultation fee for tonight, are you?"

"No, not this time. I might make you pay for dinner though!" I joked. "Talking of which shall I grab some take-away menus?"

"Great idea. All this talk is making me hungry."

Download a copy of the completed example of PERMEATE User Personas prompt sheet plus a blank template TheMysteryOfTheLostCustomer.com/Resources

---

11. "Some people need to be told to accept it and get on with it!"

We sat quietly perusing the menus when suddenly Fin broke the silence.

"You said there were a couple of things Sam struggled with. Frustration that Uma didn't 'get it' when the IT team did was the first. What was the second?"

"Sam was still feeling quite defensive saying, 'I don't think Uma would have been happy even if the onboarding had been better. Some people just need to be told to accept it and get on with it!' Before I could respond another member of the team said, 'The new supplier supported Harry with supplying the headsets in time for the team meeting and providing additional resources. Did they do the same for Uma and did it make a difference?'"

Fin was nodding. "That's true. You haven't told me whether the new supplier's approach had a more positive impact on Uma's wellbeing."

"No, I didn't. And you (and Sam) are right. A better onboarding experience doesn't guarantee product adoption. In fact, there is a difference between usage and adoption. Before I get to that, I'll tell you what Uma had to say about their onboarding experience. When Uma received the headset from the second supplier it wasn't during a team meeting like it had been for Harry's team. But they did get the additional resources, which included information about the key features of the headset and how to use them. There was also a quick-start guide specifically for their meeting platform including a 'things to look out for' section. When I asked Uma about how it made them feel they said they felt like they had been given exactly the headset they needed and all the information they needed to use it. The exact phrase was: 'It didn't feel like a hammer to crack a nut.'"

"A tick in the box for Positive Emotion and a lesson that the **'best' product isn't always the right product**," smiled Fin.

"Well deduced. In fact, I think Uma may have had a different headset to Harry's team based on the slightly different user needs. Uma also said that, with the new headset, they were able to get on with their work. No longer distracted by tech issues they were able to focus on their job and provide a good service to their customers."

"Presumably ticking the boxes for Engagement, Relationships, Expectations and Accomplishment?"

"I would say so. When, I asked if there had been any issues with the new headset. Uma said there was one but because they had details of how to get help they felt Empowered to get it resolved. And it was resolved. Quickly and with minimal impact on them doing their job."

"Another boost to their wellbeing then."

"Yes. Every experience was good and Positive Emotion was boosted. More importantly, it also built Uma's Trust in the product and the supplier. Uma was confident that help was at hand if it was needed."

"Uma would also have started rebuilding Trust with their colleagues and customers now that they were able to perform their job to an acceptable standard. So, it sounds like Uma is using the new headset, but you said product usage isn't the same as product adoption. So, what's the difference and is adoption better?"

I added to my earlier pictogram as I explained, "Onboarding is a fork in the road. It is the period between the decision to purchase and considering themselves a user. During this time they are sussing out whether the product lives up to the expectations they had. Their assessment will determine whether they take the path to compliance or the path to commitment. The path to compliance means the user will use the product but because they have to. For example, if there is no alternative or they have been told to by someone. It doesn't mean the product is bad, it just means, given the choice, the user wouldn't use it. The path to commitment means the user will use the product because they want to. They have identified the WIIFM (What's in it for me?) and are therefore bought in. The more committed to the product they are the more loyal they will be as a user."

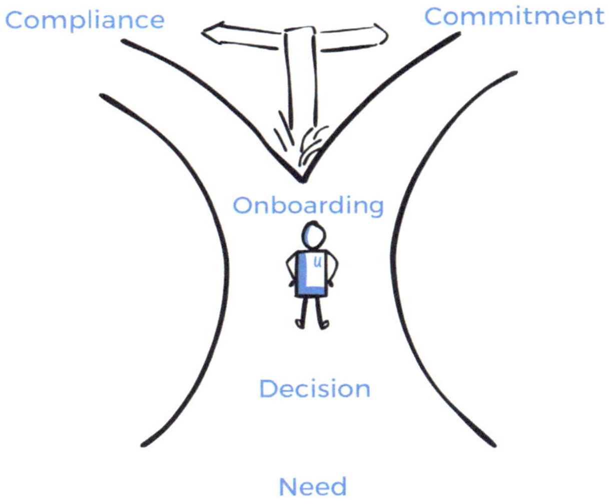

"Presumably there is a third option of not taking either path? Uma could have just thrown Sam's headset in a drawer and not used it."

"Definitely and whilst that would not have been the ideal outcome for Sam it might have been better."

"How so?"

"In the drawer the headset would have stopped impacting Uma's wellbeing, they may not have been so vocal about it and Harry's team wouldn't have heard bad things about it."

"And Harry might have gone to Clem for their headsets and Sam would have got the business. Interesting. I had never thought a customer using a product could be more damaging than not using it. It makes sense though if you consider the customer satisfaction research. The implication is that if you're a satisfied user you will tell four to five people, if you're an unhappy user you will tell nine to ten people, but if you don't consider yourself a user at all, you probably won't tell anyone. Presumably by considering user wellbeing during onboarding a user is more likely to take the path to commitment?"

"Yes. Think about using a new product as a change. We are expecting the user to be doing something different to what they have done before even if it is just using a different headset. Change is difficult for the human brain. It prefers to be on automatic pilot and continue with its old habits."

"Even when those old habits don't make them feel good?"

"Even then. Change can put the brain into a state of threat or reward. Here let me show you." I reached for a well-thumbed copy of *Neuroscience for Organizational Change*[11] from the bookcase and flicked to the required page. "On the left-hand side of the diagram, you see that the threat state sends our brains into a distracted and anxious state. The right-hand side includes positivity, focus, resilience, dopamine up. All signs of positive wellbeing."

The impact of threat and reward on our brains and on our ability to think and perform

Threat

- "Fight or flight"
- Distracted
- Anxious
- Think less clearly
- Less emotional control
- See threats where they don't exist
- See the workplace and colleagues as more hostile than they really are
- Narrower vision
- Reduce memory
- Poorer performance
- Weakened immune system
- Cortisol/stress (destroys brain cells)
- Dopamine down

Reward

- Positive
- Focused
- Resilient
- Willing to collaborate
- More able to learn – open to new ideas
- Innovative
- Creative
- Willing to get involved
- Dopamine up

"So, the onboarding experience needs to move the user towards reward."

"Exactly, and if you look at the Inverted U of performance," I said, pointing to the next diagram, "this shows the relationship between the level of arousal (or interest) and our ability to accomplish a task. You'll see impaired performance can come from too much or too little arousal.

In Uma's case the problem was too much. They were stressed out by their experience using the new headset. Another example where I see arousal being too high is when a user is bombarded with too much information at onboarding. They need enough for optimal performance. You can give them more information when they are ready and their needs have evolved."

Inverted U of Performance: Yerkes-Dodson

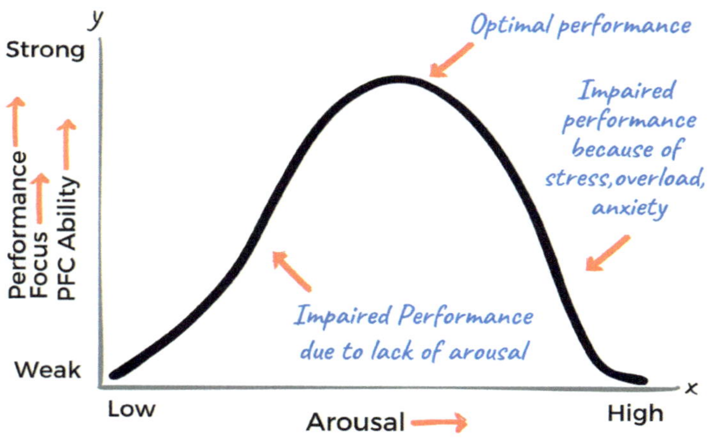

"Oh!" said Fin. "Hence why it is important to keep monitoring the stakeholders. To give them what they need when they need it. I had a customer recently that nearly went to another supplier because they didn't realise the product they had from us already had the functionality they needed."

I nodded. “That's a perfect example of how a lack of user wellbeing could Silently Kill your business and one I see far too often.”

“It's certainly a challenge that our marketing team get frustrated by despite all the product information they put out to customers but perhaps it doesn't get sent to the right people. This highlights again the importance of the difference between customers and users. So back to the chart,” Fin said turning his attention back to the book. “What would cause a user to be at the end of the curve with low arousal?”

“This could be a user who thinks the product or experience was just okay. Or, in our story, someone who didn't have the same challenges as Uma with their calls, but they were given a headset anyway and told to use it.”

“So, they joined the path at the onboarding stage without having the need?”

“Yes. So, the first step on the user path could be an actual need or a perceived need and it is an important distinction to make at the onboarding step. Whether arousal was too low or too high, the users would have been using the headsets to comply with what they had been told to do, not because they were committed to using them. The aim is to have users saying, ‘I want to use this product. I want to do it this new way,’ rather than ‘I have to use this product. I have to do it this new way.’”

“Can you use PERMEATE to help do this?”

“Of course,” I said, smiling. “Combining PERMEATE with the neuroscience of threat and reward and user personas is a really powerful tool for creating a path to product adoption."

"How do you do that?"

"For each user persona you ask the question 'What can we do to encourage a toward/reward state and avoid a threat/away state?' and assess whether it will meet the requirements for each element of PERMEATE. Before implementing any changes to meet the needs of one persona, it is important to test it against PERMEATE for the other user personas. For example, the new supplier provided a quick start guide with their headset. This would have helped Uma move towards a reward state and would tick the box for Positive Emotion, Engagement, Motivation, Expectations, Accomplishment, Trust and Empowerment."

"You missed Relationships."

"I know. The quick start guide itself probably didn't contribute to the improvement of human relationships."

"But it would have improved the relationship with the headset." interrupted Fin.

"Fair point." I smiled. "Back to cross-referencing against PERMEATE for other users, what impact would the quick reference guide have on the IT Team user persona?"

"I imagine they would be indifferent. If they didn't think they needed it they could just ignore it.

"What if reviewing the quick reference guide was mandatory before being able to use the headset?"

"Oh, that would have p!$$3d them off! Oh, and that would negatively impact their wellbeing and potentially put them in a threat or away state. You're right that could be really powerful when making decisions about the customer and user journey."

"I'm glad you think so. I will include a copy of the template with the other resources I am sending you.

Get your own copy of the PERMEATE Planning Template at TheMysteryOfTheLostCustomer.com/Resources

---

Endnotes

1. Assume makes an "ass" out of "u" and "me" is a phrase I have heard and used many times over the years. In my attempt to attribute this quote correctly, I discovered it is not clear who said it first, or when. In fact, it is not even clear what the original version of the phrase was.
2. The Power-Interest Matrix is a stakeholder analysis tool I have used for many years. Whilst it is popular amongst project managers and change managers, and widely referred to on the Internet, an original source was difficult to find. After a bit of digging it would seem the model should be attributed to Aubrey Mendelow and is sometimes called Mendelow's Matrix.
3. Hilary Scarlett, *Neuroscience for Organizational Change: An evidence-based practical guide to managing change*, 2016, Kogan Page Limited

EPILOGUE

12. "Can we get that takeaway now?"

"Wow, we have covered so much," sighed Fin. "My stomach is really rumbling. Can we get that takeaway now?"

"Great idea. Speaking of takeaways, I will place the order whilst you write down your key 'takeaways' from our discussion." Fin groaned but recognised the value in the exercise.

When I got back to Fin, they were just finishing their list.

"Here you go!" Fin said, passing me their list.

Just because one person is happy doesn't mean everyone is happy. Look beyond the customer satisfaction score.

Just because a customer has bought and received a product it doesn't mean they are using it. Ask, don't assume.

If a customer is using a product it doesn't mean they are committed to using it. Strive for adoption.

Not all customers are users and not all users are customers. Know the difference and connect with both.

Not all users are the same. Embrace diversity and be inclusive.

Beware the hidden power and interest. Seek out and monitor all stakeholders.

"These are great. They are a great starting point for a manifesto that will guide businesses who want to create meaningful and impactful products, services and experiences. It can be a reminder of their commitment to promoting wellbeing, empathy, inclusivity and growth. Can I hang on to this so I can type something up?"

"Sure. As long as you send me a copy."

"Of course."

Here is the manifesto. You can download and print a copy for your own desk from TheMysteryOfTheLostCustomer.com/Resources

---

The User Wellbeing Manifesto

1. **Beyond Customer Satisfaction:** We recognize that the happiness of one stakeholder does not guarantee wellbeing for all. We strive for holistic satisfaction to uplift everyone involved.
2. **Seek the Unseen Customers and Users:** We look for the customers and users we don't know yet. We actively search for the voices that often go unheard, ensuring their needs and wellbeing are also addressed and valued.
3. **Know, Connect, Thrive:** By understanding our customers, users, and their businesses, we create a thriving ecosystem that prioritizes their wellbeing.
4. **From Usage to Adoption:** A product is more than just a purchase; we don't assume a customer is using it just because they bought it. We go beyond mere usage and focus on fostering true adoption, unlocking the full potential of wellbeing for our users.
5. **Maximising Benefits Through Empowerment:** Just because users are using a product doesn't mean they are using it well enough to get the full benefits. We empower users with the knowledge and resources to unlock the product's full potential, enabling them to thrive.

6. **Embrace Diversity, Drive Inclusion:** We acknowledge and celebrate the uniqueness of our users, recognizing that not all users are the same. Fostering inclusivity is key to enhancing their overall wellbeing.
7. **PERMEATE a Culture of Wellbeing:** By nurturing Positive Emotion, fostering Engagement, cultivating positive Relationships, igniting Motivation, meeting Expectations, supporting Accomplishment, building Trust, and Empowering individuals, we create an environment where users, customers, and employees flourish.

"So, are you still working with Sam's company?" Fin asked.

"Yes, I check in with them on a regular basis. This new focus on user wellbeing has been a change in how the company has approached customer success in the past. I've had to be mindful of keeping all of them in a toward/reward state. That isn't always easy. Changing attitudes and behaviours takes time, support and accountability. These approaches we've been discussing are my product and I have to use PERMEATE to help my customers and users adopt them."

"I'd not thought of that," said Fin as the doorbell rang. Our food had arrived and with that the conversation moved on to more casual topics. At the end of the night, as Fin was leaving, they said, "Thanks for this evening. I feel much better than I did when I arrived. I actually feel quite motivated. Make sure you send me those resources you mentioned."

"Oh, I'm glad it has helped and, yes, I promise I will send them over. What are you going to do with them?"

"First of all I am going to take a leaf out of your book and ask to have a conversation with my customer about why we lost the business. That will help me uncover what the Silent Killer was in my case. I can use that information to assess what I could have done differently. I'm also going to share all of this with my boss. I think it would be really useful for the whole team to learn about user wellbeing and PERMEATE. We can then work together to generate ideas of how we can improve the path to product adoption and minimise the risk of user well-being Silently Killing our business in the future. Is it ok if I share your resources with my boss and the rest of the team?"

"Of course. And if you need any help, you've got my number." I winked.

A few weeks later I checked in with Fin to find out how they were getting on.

"I've really taken on board what you said. I have the manifesto pinned up on my desk and the rest of the team have been asking me about it. I've shared all your resources with the boss, and we are going to discuss them next week. I'm not sure everyone in the team will be convinced. I think they will have some of the same objections as Sam. It is already really making a difference for me though, but I guess you knew it would."

"I certainly hoped it would." I smiled. "What difference has it made?"

"I have been asking my customers better questions to understand who the stakeholders are and to get a better picture of the product users. In fact, there was one customer that contacted me to place an additional order. Instead of just fulfilling the order I asked for more information about who the extra headsets were for. It turned out they were for a very different team in the business and what I had sold them before wasn't going to be the best solution. The extra information helped me to provide not only the right product but also a better onboarding experience. If I hadn't done that I can imagine that would have been another case of the Silent Killer. The team have a lot of power and influence in the organisation."

"That's fantastic. And how did you get on with the lost customer, did you manage to speak to them?"

"Yes, I had a meeting with them last week. They were really open and honest with me and even told me who the new supplier is. It's Headsets 4 U."

I laughed out loud. I couldn't stop myself.

"What's so funny?" asked Fin.

"Well of course it's Headsets 4 U. That's who Sam works for."

Fin was silent. "This stuff really does make a difference, doesn't it?!"

"Uh-huh."

"Well, the good news is, if Sam can use these approaches to steal my customer from me, I can use the same approaches to steal them back. You know you should write a book but please don't give it to any more of my competitors."

"What a great idea!" I exclaimed.

So I did.

13. Embracing complexity: User wellbeing in the ever-evolving landscape

In this final chapter, you are invited to reflect on the journey you have taken through the simple story of a user, a customer, a supplier and a headset. You've explored the importance of understanding the distinction between customers and users, and how the concept of user wellbeing can transform the way products and services are designed, delivered and experienced.

Although the story revolves around a simple, transactional product, it is important to recognise that the world we inhabit is far from simple. Rapid technological advancements, the rise of subscription-based business models and an increasingly interconnected global marketplace have added layers of complexity to the customer and user experience. Instead of shying away from this complexity, we can embrace it. By applying the concepts introduced through this story, we can build more meaningful and enriching relationships with users, fostering loyalty and trust.

As technology continues to permeate various aspects of our existence, the focus on user wellbeing becomes all the more crucial. Balancing the allure of convenience and innovation with the potential risks to user wellbeing is a delicate task that requires ethical considerations and a profound understanding of users' needs.

The emergence of subscription-based business models has changed the dynamics of customer relationships. Instead of one-time transactions, companies now have ongoing interactions with users, making the cultivation of user wellbeing an ongoing journey. Prioritizing user success and satisfaction becomes integral to ensuring the longevity of such models.

Looking ahead, the concept of user wellbeing is not a static idea but a dynamic force that will evolve with our ever-changing world. As technology advances, we must continually reassess and adapt our strategies to meet the ever-evolving needs of users and customers alike. A user-centric approach will continue to be a key differentiator for successful businesses.

In conclusion, while the example used in our story may have been simple, the essence of user wellbeing holds a profound significance in the complex landscape of today's business world. By acknowledging and embracing this complexity, we can forge stronger connections with our users, foster sustainable growth, and ultimately create a more fulfilling and prosperous future for all.

WHO IS SUSANNAH SIMMONS?

Hi, I'm Susannah Simmons, the Software Adoption Doctor.

I fell into IT training over twenty years ago after graduating from Plymouth university with my degree in business studies. I started out training on MS Office applications before moving on to more niche customer experience products and processes. I have worked in a wide range of industries including software, new homes, financial services, public sector, marketing and charities.

I am a big supporter of digital transformation and I firmly believe that, to be successful, the tools need to be considered in the context of the processes and the people. This means that, whether doing the work myself (I like to get my hands dirty from time to time), or coaching others to do it, my past projects have focused on change management, stakeholder engagement, business analysis, project management, communication, training design and delivery including supporting resources and documentation.

I am considered and empathic. I actively listen and put myself in the stakeholder's shoes to design and deliver programmes that satisfy all their needs. I help users to feel excited about their new tools and processes and to feel confident, competent and committed to the change.

When I am not being the Software Adoption Doctor, you will find me helping people get fit and stay fit as the Feel Good Fitness Coach or spending time with the 'Gourmet Globetrotters' my husband (Dom) and my daughter (Harriet).

SOME WAYS TO TAKE THINGS FURTHER

Things you can do on your own

- Explore the book's resources at TheMysteryOfTheLostCustomer.com/Resources and check back frequently as new resources are added.
- Use the resources with your team to identify opportunities for you to better understand your users and customers and improve their wellbeing.

To help you share the story of Uma the user, Clem the customer and Sam the supplier with others, you can download The Mystery of the Lost Customer picture book at TheMysteryOfTheLostCustomer.com/Resources

---

If you want support

If you would like help learning and applying the concepts I introduce in the book. Here are three ways we could work together:

1. **Individuals**
   Through one-to-one coaching, I can help you think through and apply the concepts to your specific situation to help you retain customers and grow recurring revenues.
2. **Teams**
   Through education and workshops, together we can help your customer-facing teams to apply the concepts of user-wellbeing to build more meaningful and enriching relationships with users and customers, fostering loyalty and trust.
3. **Organisations**
   If you are part of a business, association or community that aims to inspire and motivate people and encourage them to take action or adopt new ideas you can book me as a speaker as part of your next event or initiative.

ACKNOWLEDGEMENTS

Top of my list is my husband Dom. Words cannot express how grateful I am for his endless support over the years as I have pursued my dreams as a multi-passionate entrepreneur. A very close second is our daughter, Harriet, who tolerates the love I have for what I do. I hope, if nothing else, I can inspire her to follow her dreams whatever they may be.

Special thanks go to Debs Jenkins (my book writing mentor) and Dan Kowalski (my book writing buddy) who helped me realise that the book I planned to write was not the book I really needed and wanted to write. They cheered me on, and picked me up, when the imposter gremlins came to call. Without their unwavering support this book would never have been written.

I also want to express my gratitude to Clare Muscutt and her amazing community, Women in CX.[12] They gave me the opportunity to tell the story of Uma, Clem and Sam for the first time and test the concept of User Wellbeing as a Silent Killer in business.

Last, but by no means least, thank you to my beta readers Mike Grocott and Emma Williams, my editor Lisa de Caux and my designer Jayr Cuario. They challenged my assumptions about my users (readers) and helped me refine the book and shape it into something worth publishing.

Endnotes

1. Women in CX is the world's first membership community for women in customer experience and technology. Their mission is to bring these women together from across the globe to network, overcome shared challenges and amplify their voices. https://womenincx.community/

9781908770431
BV - #0005 - 040424 - C78 - 203/127/5 - PB - 9781908770431 - Matt Lamination